THE BIKER COOKBOOK

Spuds Murphy

Gramercy Books • New York

This edition is published by Gramercy
Books™, an imprint of Random House
Value Publishing, Inc., 201 East 50th
Street, New York, N.Y. 10022.

Gramercy Books™ and design are
trademarks of Random House Value
Publishing

Random House
New York • Toronto • London • Sydney •
Auckland

http://www.randomhouse.com/

The author wishes to thank the following
for their help in preparing this book:
Larry A. Dannlevith, Joseph F. Ferrino,
Chris Guerra, Frank Guerra, Ed McDevitt,
Regina McLoughlin, John Neuer, Brian
Pratt, Adam Schmitt, Lori Sirgiovanni,
Anthony Vicari, Lenny Weber, Jr.

Cover design by Jeff Faust
Text design by Melissa Campbell
and Robert Yaffe
Front cover photograph of bikers
© WORKBOOK CO/OP STOCK/
Robert Mizono 1998.

Printed and bound in Malaysia.

A CIP catalog record for this book is
available from the Library of Congress.

ISBN 0-517-20565-3

9 8 7 6 5 4 3 2

CONTENTS

BREAKFAST

BARBECUED OMELETTE

🏍

JOHN HENRY'S HOT & SPICY OMELETTE

🏍

CURLY'S HIP-HUGGING CINNAMON BUNS

🏍

UNCLE BEAU'S BLUEBERRY PANCAKES

🏍

GRITS, REDEYE GRAVY & HAM

🏍

HUMDINGER HASH BROWNS

🏍

CLASSIC CORN PONE

🏍

MORNING BISCUITS

🏍

ARMADILLO SAL'S FRITTATA

🏍

NUTS & BOLTS ORANGE BREAD

🏍

OATMEAL BLUEBERRY MUFFINS

Barbecued Omelette

4 eggs
¼ cup milk or water
1 Tbsp oil
½ onion, chopped
½ cup cooked, barbecued meat (leftover ribs, scraped off bone)
2 Tbsp barbecue sauce
Dash hot pepper sauce
Salt and pepper to taste

Sauté onion in the oil in a frying pan; add the meat, barbecue sauce, and hot sauce, and stir until heated. In a bowl, beat eggs with milk or water, and season with salt and pepper. In another frying pan, add eggs and when they begin to set, add barbecue mixture and fold over to make omelette. Serve with any extra barbecue sauce on top.

John Henry's Hot & Spicy Omelette

3 eggs, lightly beaten
½ cup chopped onion
½ green pepper, chopped
2 large tomatoes, chopped
1 clove garlic, mashed
1 tsp fresh basil, chopped or ½ tsp dried basil
1 tsp fresh cilantro, chopped
½ tsp chopped jalapeño pepper
½ cup Monterey Jack cheese, shredded
1 Tbsp oil
Salt and pepper to taste

Heat about half the oil in a medium saucepan. Sauté the onions, garlic, green peppers, jalapeño peppers, and tomatoes until soft. In a skillet, heat the remaining oil and add the eggs. When they begin to set and the undersides are lightly browned, flip over. Add vegetable filling; then add cheese, basil, and cilantro. Season with salt and pepper. Fold in half and cook on low until cheese melts.

Curly's Hip-Hugging Cinnamon Buns

1 box buttermilk biscuit mix (do not use refrigerated dough mix)
6 Tbsp softened butter or stick margarine
6 Tbsp brown sugar, crumbled finely
½ tsp cinnamon, or to taste

Make the dough according to package directions and chill. Roll out the dough into a rectangle or square about 1/3 inch thick. Slightly dampen a paper towel and brush it over the top surface to remove excess flour. Spread butter evenly over the top and sprinkle on all the brown sugar and the cinnamon. Roll up dough and slice into 2/3-inch rounds. Bake as directed on the box.

"Live life full throttle. Ride a chopper."

— Bubba Longman

Uncle Beau's Blueberry Pancakes

2 cups flour
3 tsp baking powder
½ tsp salt
¼ cup sugar
2 eggs
2 Tbsp oil
1 cup milk
1 cup blueberries

Sift dry ingredients in bowl and add blueberries. Stir in liquid ingredients with whisk or spoon until mixed. Do not over mix. Rub skillet with oil and heat until water drops bounce. Drop pancakes into skillet with large mixing spoon or soup ladle. When bubbles appear at the top of the pancakes, flip them and brown the other side. Keep the skillet hot at all times.

You may substitute other fruits and/or pecans or walnut pieces instead of the blueberries. Be sure to add them before you stir in the liquid; this will keep them more evenly distributed in the pancakes.

Grits, Redeye Gravy & Ham

6 servings of grits
6 country ham slices
½ cup brewed coffee
Ham drippings

Prepare the grits according to package directions. In an ungreased frying pan, cook ham slices until browned, approximately 5-6 minutes each side. Remove from skillet. Pour off all but 2 tablespoons of drippings from pan. Add coffee and cook over medium heat for 2-3 minutes, scraping pan to pick up flavorful bits of ham. Spoon coffee mixture over hot cooked grits and serve with warm ham.

Humdinger Hash Browns

5 potatoes
1 large onion, chopped
½ green pepper, chopped
⅓-½ cup vegetable oil
Salt and pepper to taste

Peel potatoes and cut into 1/4-inch slices or cubes. Reserve in bowl of cold water until ready to use. Heat large frying pan to medium high and add oil. Drain potatoes and pat dry. Add potatoes to hot oil. Cover and cook for about 10 minutes, turning potatoes when browned. Add onions and green peppers. Cook covered until potatoes are soft and onions are cooked through. Season with salt and pepper.

Classic Corn Pone

1 cup cornmeal
1 tsp baking powder
½ tsp baking soda
2 Tbsp butter or margarine
½ cup milk
Oil or margarine for frying

Mix dry ingredients together. Cut in butter or margarine with pastry blender or fingers until mixture is crumbly. Slowly add milk until dough forms. Grease a hot skillet and drop dough by spoonful onto skillet until cooked through. Good with jam or honey, and more butter (if you want!).

Morning Biscuits

2 cups flour
½ tsp salt
1 tsp sugar
¼ tsp baking soda
1 Tbsp baking powder
5 Tbsp shortening
1 cup buttermilk

Preheat oven to 425°. Sift dry ingredients. Cut in the shortening with a pastry blender or your hands until the mixture resembles coarse cornmeal. Make a well in the middle of the mixture and pour in buttermilk. Mix just until ingredients are combined, and a soft dough is formed. Do not over mix. On a lightly floured surface, knead the dough gently until it is soft and elastic (not sticky). Pat dough out until about 1/2-inch thick. Cut circles with a cookie cutter or drinking glass. Place the biscuits 1/2-inch apart on lightly greased baking sheet for a crisp-crusted biscuit or touching each other for a softer biscuit. Bake for 12-15 minutes.

Armadillo Sal's Frittata

4 medium potatoes, peeled and sliced
1 lb sausage, crumbled
6 eggs
¼ cup milk
1 cup grated sharp Cheddar cheese
1 4-oz can chopped green chile peppers
1 medium onion, chopped
Oil for frying
Salt and pepper to taste
Prepared salsa

Place sliced potatoes in pot with water and cook until almost done. Drain. Meanwhile, fry sausage in skillet. Remove sausage and drain. Add onions and cook until tender. Add enough oil to skillet to brown potatoes. Drain off excess oil, leaving about 2 tablespoons. Add chopped green chile peppers and sausage to skillet and mix well. In a bowl, combine eggs and milk and beat until mixed. Add salt and pepper to taste. Pour eggs over sausage, onion and potato mixture in skillet. Cook over low heat, gently lifting potatoes to allow eggs to cook.

Turn on the broiler. After frittata seems to be cooked in the bottom of the skillet, sprinkle Cheddar cheese on top. Place skillet inside broiler and broil until cheese is bubbly. Serve frittata by the slice topped with salsa. Serve with bread of your choice.

Nuts & Bolts Orange Bread

2 Tbsp butter or margarine
½ cup boiling water
2 cups sifted flour
1 tsp baking soda
1 tsp baking powder
½ tsp salt
½ cup orange juice
2 Tbsp grated orange rind
1 cup granulated sugar
2 tsp vanilla extract
1 egg, lightly beaten
½ cup chopped nuts

Preheat oven to 350°. In medium size heat-proof bowl, melt butter or margarine in boiling water. Sift flour, soda, baking powder, and salt together. Add orange juice, grated rind, sugar, and vanilla to butter mixture. Add egg. Sift flour mixture over orange mix, add nuts, and stir until moist (batter will be lumpy). Pour into greased and floured 4 x 8 loaf pan. Bake 1 hour. Remove from pan and cool on wire rack. Store in waxed paper.

Oatmeal Blueberry Muffins

1¼ cups quick-cooking oatmeal
1 cup flour
⅓ cup granulated sugar
1 Tbsp baking powder
½ tsp salt
1 cup milk
1 egg
¼ cup vegetable oil
1 cup blueberries, rinsed and drained

Preheat oven to 425°. Combine oats, flour, sugar, baking powder, and salt. Mix in milk, egg, and oil, stirring gently until just moist. Fold in blueberries. Fill greased muffin tins 2/3 full with batter. Bake for 20 to 25 minutes. Makes 1 dozen.

APPETIZERS

CAJUN-STYLE BUFFALO WINGS

GRILLED CHILE-LIME WINGS

MOZZARELLA CHEESE STICKS

BLACK-EYED PEA DIP

GUACAMOLE DIP

LITTLE DOGS

MIGHTY MEATY DIP

TEX-MEX CHEESE DIP

TEXAS CAVIAR

MONTEZUMA'S MOUNTAIN

CALAMARI SALAD

FINGER-LICKIN' CHICKEN
FINGERS WITH SAUCE

Cajun-Style Buffalo Wings

3-4 lbs chicken wings
½-1 tsp cayenne pepper
¼ tsp salt
2 tsp black pepper
½ tsp minced onion
2 garlic cloves, crushed
1 8-oz bottle spicy
   barbecue sauce
2 Tbsp jalapeño sauce
1 Tbsp hot sauce
1 Tbsp Cajun spice or
   Cajun seasoning mix

Combine chicken wings, sauces, and all spices in large saucepan. Cover and heat on low for several hours until chicken is cooked through.

Purée the canned chile peppers in a blender. Mix all ingredients together in a bowl and marinate for 2-3 hours maximum. Heat grill and cook wings, basting with saved marinade until done.

Grilled Chile-Lime Wings

5 lbs chicken
   wings
1 cup lime juice
1 4-oz can
   chopped
   green chile
   peppers
2 Tbsp garlic powder
   or 3 cloves garlic, crushed
2 Tbsp paprika
1 Tbsp sugar
2 Tbsp salt
1 Tbsp lemon-pepper seasoning
1 Tbsp soy sauce
¼ cup olive oil or vegetable oil

"Harness your thunder. Hug a biker."

— Billy "Butterball" Smith

Mozzarella Cheese Sticks

1 lb packaged mozzarella cheese
2 eggs, beaten
½ cup flour
1 cup flavored bread crumbs
Vegetable oil for frying

Slice the mozzarella into flat wedges or strips. Prepare 1 bowl with flour, one bowl with beaten eggs, and 1 bowl with bread crumbs. Take each mozzarella strip and coat with flour, beaten egg, and then bread crumbs. Immediately after coating, fry each stick in hot oil (about 1/4-inch deep) for one or two minutes on each side until breading is golden brown and cheese is melted. Note: in order to get the best results, fry the coated sticks as soon as possible while coating is still fresh and don't let the oil get too hot during frying.

This recipe also can be used with zucchini, peppers, and other vegetables.

jalapeño pepper. Mash mixture until chunky. Add cheese. Stir over low heat until the cheese is melted. Serve warm with tortilla chips.

Guacamole Dip

1 cup sour cream
1 14-oz can black beans, drained
1 cup chopped onion
1 avocado
3 Tbsp mayonnaise
1 tsp lemon juice
1 garlic clove, crushed
1 cup chopped fresh tomato
Salt and pepper to taste
Vegetable oil for frying

Sauté 3/4 cup onion in vegetable oil and add the black beans. Simmer for 2-3 minutes, stirring frequently. Pour beans into a serving bowl and let cool. Add layer of sour cream. In a separate bowl, peel the avocado, remove pit, and coarsely mash. Add the remaining onion, garlic, mayonnaise, and lemon juice. Add salt and pepper to taste. Mix (or use a

Black-Eyed Pea Dip

2 cups canned black-eyed peas
3 Tbsp bacon drippings
1 8-oz can tomatoes or 2 peeled
   fresh tomatoes
1 cup chopped onion
1 Tbsp chopped jalapeño pepper
½ cup grated sharp Cheddar
   cheese
Salt and pepper to taste

In a saucepan, sauté the onion in the bacon drippings. Add peas, tomatoes, and

processor) until the guacamole is smooth. Add the guacamole to the serving dish. Top with remaining sour cream and chopped tomato. Serve with tortilla chips.

Little Dogs

½ lb hot dogs cut into bite-sized chunks (or cocktail franks)
1 cup ketchup
1 cup whiskey
1 cup brown sugar
1 small onion, chopped

In a saucepan or casserole dish combine all ingredients. Simmer on low for 2 hours. Serve warm.

Mighty Meaty Dip

½ lb lean ground beef
½ lb pork sausage
1 lb process Cheddar cheese
1 cup finely chopped onion
1 cup chunky salsa (your choice, mild or hot)
½ can cream of mushroom soup
2 large garlic cloves, minced

Combine beef and sausage together and cook until browned and crumbly. Drain on paper towels. In a large frying pan, combine meat mixture and remaining ingredients. Cook and stir over low heat until cheese is melted. Serve warm with pita bread or tortilla chips.

Tex-Mex Cheese Dip

1 lb process Cheddar cheese, cubed
1 lb process Cheddar cheese spread
½ cup finely chopped onion
1 4-oz can chopped green chile peppers
1 Tbsp butter

In a large saucepan, cook onions and butter over medium heat until onions become clear. Add both cheeses and stir until melted. Add green chile peppers and heat through. Serve warm.

Texas Caviar

2 cups canned black-eyed peas
1 4-oz can chopped green chile peppers
2 tomatoes, seeded and diced
1 green pepper, chopped
1 clove garlic, minced
2 Tbsp minced onion
2 Tbsp chopped celery
1/4 cup olive oil
2 Tbsp cider vinegar
Dash of cayenne pepper or hot sauce
Parsley and fresh cilantro to taste
Salt and pepper to taste

Wash and drain peas well and set aside. Combine chile peppers, tomatoes, peppers, garlic, onions, and celery. Stir in oil and vinegar. Season to taste with the remaining ingredients. Pour over peas and stir gently. Refrigerate for several hours or overnight. Serve with corn chips.

Montezuma's Mountain

1 15-oz can refried bean dip
2 ripe avocados
1 tsp cumin
1 Tbsp lemon juice
black pepper to taste
garlic powder to taste
1 can pitted black olives, chopped
½ medium onion, chopped
2 4-oz cans green chile peppers
2 tomatoes, diced
2 cups sour cream
1 cup grated Cheddar cheese
1 cup salsa

Line serving dish or bowl with bean dip. Mash avocado and mix with cumin, lemon juice, pepper and garlic powder. Spread on top of bean dip. Add layers of other ingredients in the following order:

onions, chile peppers, tomatoes, olives, salsa, sour cream, and cheese. Serve with crackers, tortilla chips, or other chips.

Calamari Salad

1 lb small or medium-sized squid, prepared
1¼ cup dry white wine
1 scallion, chopped
Strip of lemon peel
1 garlic clove, chopped
1 red onion, chopped
¼ cup mixed fresh herbs, such as basil, tarragon, and Italian parsley
Fresh herb sprigs

Dressing:
5 Tbsp olive oil
2 Tbsp lemon juice
1 tsp balsamic vinegar
1 tsp Dijon-style mustard
Salt and freshly ground pepper

In a medium-size saucepan, bring to a boil the wine, scallion, lemon peel and garlic. Add the squid, in batches, and cook 5 to 7 minutes until firm but still tender. Using a slotted spoon removed to a serving dish and cool. Add onion and herbs to squid and mix.

To make dressing, mix all ingredients together in a small bowl or shake together in a jar with a tight-fitting lid. Pour over salad and toss to mix. Cover and refrigerate at least 30 minutes before serving. Garnish with fresh herbs.

Finger-Lickin' Chicken Fingers with Sauce

4 boneless and skinless chicken breasts
2 Tbsp plain yogurt
15 plain saltine crackers, crushed
1 tsp dried thyme
½ tsp dried marjoram
¼ tsp curry powder
Salt to taste

Sauce:
   ½ cup plain yogurt
   2 Tbsp ketchup
   2 Tbsp finely chopped celery
   2 tsp soy sauce
   Black pepper to taste
   Finely chopped garlic (optional)

Preheat oven to 375°. Trim fat from chicken and cut each breast into strips. Coat chicken pieces with yogurt. Combine cracker crumbs and spices on a plate and roll chicken strips in crumbs. Refrigerate chicken for one hour. Bake chicken on a lightly-oiled rack set into a baking pan for 25 minutes until crumbs are lightly browned. Combine all ingredients for sauce and serve as a dip.

MAIN DISHES

SHREDDED BEEF BURRITOS

BLACK BEAN CHILI

BEEF TORTILLA

CLASSIC BARBECUED SPARERIBS

DEEP SOUTH BARBECUE SAUCE

CHICKEN-FRIED STEAK

BUST-A-GUT MEATBALL HERO

LOUISIANA PO' BOY

MOTORMOUTH CREOLE BURGER

CORNDOGS

CHILI DAWGS

SPIKE'S MEATLOAF

LOWRIDER BEEF PICADILLO

BB'S PORK CHOPS

SILVER BULLET CHICKEN NUGGETS

BARBECUED CHICKEN

SWEETHEART CHICKEN

HOT HOT HOT CHICKEN THIGHS

CHICK 'N' CHILI

FLAKY CHICKEN

CHICKEN JAMBALAYA

CHICKEN WITH BISCUITS

BOURBON CHICKEN

SPICY FISH FILLETS

CREOLE FISH FRY

SOAKED SHRIMP

BREWERY SHRIMP

SEAFOOD ROLLS

LINGUINE WITH SHRIMP SAUCE

CAJUN CRAWFISH STEW

BARBECUED SHRIMP

BLACKENED CATFISH

GRILLED SHRIMP

SPAGHETTI & MEAT SAUCE

MACARONI & CHEESE

LAST GASP LASAGNA

TOTAL PIZZA

Shredded Beef Burritos

1 lb boneless beef chuck roast
1 medium onion, chopped
4 garlic cloves
1 tsp dried oregano
1 tsp dried cumin
1½ cups water
Salt and pepper to taste
Olive oil
1 cup finely chopped onion
4 garlic cloves, crushed
1 medium tomato, chopped
1 tsp ground cumin
2 tsp cilantro
2 Tbsp chopped canned chile peppers
6 to 8 flour tortillas

Place beef in large pot. Add the 6 following ingredients and bring to a boil. Reduce heat, cover, and simmer for 1½ hours or until beef is tender and falling apart. Heat oil in large frying pan and sauté onions until soft. Add garlic and cook an additional minute. Add the tomato and chile peppers and cook about 2 minutes. Add the shredded beef and seasonings, stir well and cook over medium heat until hot. Divide the fillings among the tortillas and wrap tightly.

Black Bean Chili

1 Tbsp vegetable oil
1½ lbs lean, boneless round steak or chuck cut into 3/4-inch pieces
1 large onion, chopped
1 large green pepper, chopped
2 cloves garlic, minced
2 14-oz can plum tomatoes
1 14-oz can chicken broth (low-salt is best)
1 4-oz can chopped green chile peppers
1¼ ounce package chili seasoning mix
3 12-oz cans black beans, drained and rinsed
Sour cream
Fresh chopped cilantro

Heat oil in a large Dutch oven over medium-high until hot. Add steak; cook 6-8 minutes, until meat is browned. Add onion, garlic, chiles, and seasoning mix and cook until onion is tender. Add tomatoes and broth. Bring to a boil, reduce heat, cover and simmer 1/2 hour, stirring occasionally. Add beans, cover and simmer 10 minutes more. Garnish each serving with sour cream and cilantro. Serve with rice.

Beef Tortilla

¾ cup chopped onion
1 lb lean ground sirloin
1 tsp chili powder
1 clove garlic, minced
2 tsp jalapeño peppers
2 tomatoes, sliced thin
½ tsp cumin
1 Tbsp fresh cilantro
½ green pepper, sliced thin
¼ onion, sliced thin
4 oz shredded Cheddar cheese
2 cups shredded iceberg lettuce
4 10-inch flour tortillas
4 Tbsp sour cream
Salt and pepper to taste

Heat a skillet and sauté the beef until brown. Push the beef aside and add the chopped onion and garlic. Sauté until softened. Mix with the beef. Add the jalapeño pepper, cilantro, cumin, chili powder, salt and pepper. Stir to blend well. In a separate frying pan, heat the tortillas. Divide the beef into the 4 tortillas. Divide the tomatoes, lettuce, sliced onion, cheese, green pepper and sour cream evenly among the tortillas. Roll each tortilla tightly.

Classic Barbecued Spareribs

4 lbs pork spareribs
2 medium onions, sliced
2 tsp salt
¼ tsp pepper
1 8-oz can crushed tomatoes
1 4-oz can tomato paste
2 Tbsp brown sugar
¾ cup water
2 Tbsp vinegar
2 tsp Worcestershire sauce
⅛ tsp cayenne
1 tsp chili powder

Preheat oven to 350°. Arrange spareribs in large baking dish. Add onions and sprinkle with salt and pepper. Combine remaining ingredients and pour over spareribs. Cover and bake in medium oven about 1-1/2 hours, basting frequently. Remove cover and bake 20 minutes longer. Can also be made with beef spareribs.

Deep South Barbecue Sauce

8 cups water
1½ cups brown sugar
1½ cups Worcestershire sauce
1½ cups prepared yellow mustard
1 quart ketchup
¼ cup pepper
¼ cup red pepper flakes
12 cups red wine vinegar
4 cups white table wine
1½ cups salt

Mix all ingredients in a casserole dish or non-aluminum saucepan. Bring to a boil and then simmer for 30 minutes. Store in glass jar. Makes 2 gallons.

Chicken-Fried Steak

¼ cup flour
½ tsp garlic salt
Pinch of cayenne pepper
Black pepper to taste
4 rump or round steaks, 6-oz each and about ½-inch thick
2 Tbsp vegetable oil or beef drippings

Combine the flour, salt, and cayenne pepper in a bag and shake. Add steaks and shake to coat. Heat the oil or drippings in a large skillet over medium-high heat. Add the steaks and fry 3 minutes on each side for rare and 5 minutes on each side for well done, adding oil as needed. Remove steaks from pan and gradually add flour mixture from bag to pan drippings. Stir, scraping pan bottom and adding hot water if necessary. Stir continuously until gravy thickens and bubbles.

Bust-a-Gut Meatball Hero

1 lb lean ground beef
5 Tbsp grated Romano cheese
1 medium onion, grated
2 cloves garlic, crushed
2 Tbsp fresh chopped Italian parsley
1 egg, beaten
3 slices white bread, crust removed
¼ cup milk
Fresh ground black pepper to taste
2 cups tomato sauce, homemade or canned
Olive oil
4 Italian sub or hero rolls

Tear the white bread into small pieces and soak in bowl with milk for a few minutes. Add the ground beef, onion, garlic, cheese, parsley, egg, and pepper and mix with your hands until blended well. Roll the meat into about 16 balls. Heat a thin layer of olive oil in a pan. When the oil is hot, add the meatballs and brown on all sides. Remove to a platter lined with paper towels and drain. Put the meatballs in a saucepan and pour tomato sauce to cover. Simmer covered for 20 minutes. Slice rolls in half and fill with meatballs and sauce.

Louisiana Po' Boy

6 Tbsp butter or margarine
6 Tbsp flour
1 large onion, sliced
1 small green pepper, sliced
1 small red pepper, sliced
2 cups beef broth
1 tsp Worcestershire sauce
¾ tsp hot sauce
½ tsp dried thyme, crushed
1 lb cooked roast beef, thinly sliced
4 sub or hero rolls

Melt butter in medium saucepan. Add onion and green pepper and cook over medium heat. Stir in flour. Cook, stirring constantly, until flour browns, about 3 minutes. Gradually stir in broth. Add Worcestershire sauce, hot sauce and thyme and stir constantly until mixture boils and thickens. Slice each roll in half lengthwise and scoop out soft insides. Arrange meat on each roll, spoon extra gravy over meat, and replace tops on rolls.

Motormouth Creole Burger

2 lbs ground chuck
¾ cup mayonnaise
1 Tbsp hot creole mustard
1 tsp hot creole spices
16 tomato slices
16 red onion slices
2 Tbsp Creole marinade
8 slices Monterey Jack cheese
8 hamburger rolls

In a bowl, mix mayonnaise and mustard until blended. Cover and refrigerate for 30 minutes. In another bowl, gently toss tomato and onion slices in creole marinade to coat. Cover for 30 minutes and drain excess liquid. Form beef into 8 patties and shake creole spices on both sides of each patty. Broil or grill burger to desired doneness. Top each burger with a slice of cheese and allow cheese to melt. Spread bottom of each bun with mustard-mayonnaise mixture, add burger with the cheese and top each with 2 tomato slices and 2 onion slices.

Corndogs

6 hot dogs
1 cup pancake mix
1 cup cornmeal
Water as needed
Oil for frying

Mix pancake and cornmeal together and add enough water to reach a desired batter consistency. Dip hot dogs into batter, making sure the ends are covered with batter and no hot dog is showing. Heat oil to medium high. Drop batter-dipped dogs into oil and cook until golden brown. Remove from pan and lay on paper towels to remove excess grease.

Chili Dawgs

12 hot dogs
1 lb lean ground beef
½ tsp Worcestershire sauce
¼ tsp prepared Dijon-style mustard
¼ tsp dried oregano
½ cup water
1 small onion, minced
2 8-oz cans tomato sauce
1 tsp chili powder
¼ tsp garlic powder
Salt to taste

Brown the ground beef in a large saucepan over medium heat. Add the Worcestershire sauce, mustard, and oregano and stir. Add the remaining ingredients and continue to stir. Reduce heat, add the hot dogs, and simmer for about 15 minutes.

Spike's Meatloaf

2½ lbs ground beef
1 tsp cayenne pepper
1 tsp oregano
½ cup fine bread crumbs
2 cloves garlic, crushed
½ small onion, chopped
1 tsp dried thyme
1 tsp dried basil
¼ tsp cumin
1 tsp mustard powder
1 tsp soy sauce
1 tsp Worcestershire sauce

Preheat oven to 300°. Put meat and onion in a bowl. Mix everything else together

and then add to meat and onion. Mix well and shape into a loaf pan. Spices may be adjusted to taste, increasing the cayenne to really spice it up. Bake for about 1½ hours. Cool and slice.

Lowrider Beef Picadillo

3-1/2 lbs lean ground beef
6 onions, chopped
3 cloves garlic, chopped
3 Tbsp oil
9 Tbsp vinegar
1 64-oz can tomatoes
2 tsp ground cloves
2 Tbsp ground cumin
1-1/2 Tbsp sugar
2 Tbsp cinnamon
1 8-oz can corn
6-8 oz slivered almonds
1 small can pitted ripe black olives, chopped
6 tsp salt
1 4-oz can chile peppers, drained and chopped

2 Tbsp tomato paste
1/2 cup seedless raisins (optional)
1 lb. grated Cheddar cheese
Crisp lettuce, shredded

Cook garlic and onions in oil. Add meat and brown. Add all remaining ingredients except almonds, olives, cheese, lettuce, and raisins. Heat to boiling. Reduce heat and simmer one hour or more. Stir in almonds, olives, and raisins if desired. Just before serving add cheese and allow it to melt. Serve with shredded lettuce.

BB's Pork Chops

6 thick-cut pork chops
1 12-oz can beer
1 cup ketchup
²⁄₃ cup brown sugar
1 tsp mustard powder

Preheat oven to 350°. Brown chops in skillet. Mix remaining ingredients together. Layer chops in a baking dish and pour sauce over top. Bake 1-1½ hours until chops are tender.

Silver Bullet Chicken Nuggets

2 pounds chicken, skinned and boned
½ lb pork sausage
3 cups fresh bread crumbs
3 eggs
½ tsp salt
⅛ tsp pepper
Flour
Oil for frying
½ cup pineapple preserves
2 Tbsp hot or sweet mustard

Finely chop chicken. Combine chicken, sausage, 1 cup of bread crumbs, 1 egg, salt and pepper. Mix well and form into 1-inch balls. Lightly beat the remaining eggs. Set up 3 bowls: one with flour, one with beaten eggs and one with remaining bread crumbs. Roll chicken nuggets in

each bowl, beginning with flour, then eggs, and bread crumbs. Chill for several hours. Heat oil for shallow frying (½ inch). Fry chicken nuggets until golden brown. Drain on paper towels. Prepare sauce by cooking preserves and mustard slowly over low heat, stirring frequently. Serve nuggets hot or at room temperature with mustard sauce or dip of choice.

Fiery Barbecued Chicken

2-3 lbs chicken, cut into eighths
¼ cup bacon drippings
1 Tbsp maple syrup
1 cup chopped onion
4 large cloves garlic, minced
1 44-oz bottle ketchup
¼ cup cider vinegar
¼ cup dark molasses
¼ cup Worcestershire sauce
½ cup flat beer
2 Tbsp Dijon-style mustard
1 tbsp liquid smoke
1 tsp hot pepper sauce
1 tsp ground black pepper
1 Tbsp finely minced jalapeño peppers

Melt bacon drippings in a heavy 3-quart saucepan. Add onion and garlic, and cook about 3 minutes. Add maple syrup, ketchup, vinegar, molasses, Worcestershire sauce, beer, mustard, and stir well. Add remaining ingredients, stir well, cover and simmer 30 minutes.

Preheat oven to 400°. Place chicken pieces, skin side up, in 2 large, shallow roasting pans. Bake 30-40 minutes, then turn pieces over and reduce oven to 350°. Baste each chicken piece with sauce, using about 3 cups of the sauce. Bake 15 minutes. Turn chicken and baste with 1 more cup sauce. Bake 20 to 30 minutes longer or until sauce is glazed and tips of chicken pieces are lightly browned.

Sweetheart Chicken

3 lb broiler/fryer chicken, skinned
1 cup shredded yellow squash
1 cup shredded zucchini
1 cup finely chopped onion
1 cup finely chopped celery
1¼ cup toasted bread crumbs
1 clove garlic, crushed
1 egg, beaten
¼ cup chopped pecans
¼ tsp salt
¼ tsp pepper
3 Tbsp unsweetened apple juice
2 Tbsp honey

Preheat oven to 350°. Clean and rinse chicken and pat dry. Coat a large skillet with oil and heat to medium-high. Add yellow squash, zucchini, onion, celery and garlic and sauté until tender but crisp. Drain. In a medium bowl, combine vegetable mixture with bread crumbs, egg, pecans, salt and pepper to taste, and stir well.

Place chicken, breast side up, on a rack in a greased roasting pan. Lightly stuff with dressing mixture. Combine apple juice and honey, stirring well. Brush chicken with half the mixture and bake at 350° for 1 to 1½ hours or until drumsticks are easy to move and juices run clear. Baste occasionally with remaining honey mixture.

Hot Hot Hot Chicken Thighs

1½–2 lbs chicken thighs, skinned
¼ cup Caribbean-style hot sauce
¼ cup lime juice
¼ cup yellow mustard
2 Tbsp wine vinegar
2 Tbsp chopped parsley
2 Tbsp dried thyme
¼ tsp dried ginger
Salt and pepper to taste

Score chicken on both sides by making diagonal cuts about 1 inch apart. In a large mixing bowl, blender or food processor, mix hot sauce, lime juice, mustard and vinegar. Add spices and blend until mixture forms a saucy paste.

Mix chicken thighs with pasta to coat chicken. Marinate in refrigerator for 2-8 hours, turning chicken occasionally to coat. Remove chicken and reserve sauce.

Place chicken on uncovered grill and grill directly over medium heat for approximately 15 minutes. Turn chicken and grill for about 10 to 15 minutes more. Baste both sides with reserved marinade and grill for 5 minutes more, or until chicken is tender and no pink remains. Discard remaining marinade.

Chick 'n' Chili

2 lbs boneless, skinless chicken breasts
1 lb navy beans, soaked overnight
1 medium onion, chopped
3 cloves garlic, minced
2 4-oz cans green chile peppers
2 tsp ground cumin
1 tsp dried oregano
1½ tsp cayenne pepper
1 14-oz can chicken broth
1 cup water
Salt to taste

Drain beans and rinse off. Put beans in medium pan and cover with water. Bring to a boil. Reduce heat and simmer 30 minutes. Discard water. Cut chicken into 1-inch pieces and brown. Put all ingredients in large pot and mix thoroughly. Cover. Cook on low heat for 1½ -2 hours until chicken and beans are cooked through.

Flaky Chicken

1 frying chicken,
    cut up
½ cup milk
1 egg, beaten
2 cups crushed
    cornflakes
2 tsp salt
1 tsp paprika
2 tsp black pepper
½ teaspoon dried sage
½ teaspoon dried
    tarragon
Oil for frying

Combine milk and egg in a large bowl and set aside. Combine cornflakes, herbs, and spices in paper or plastic bag. Add a few pieces of chicken at a time to the bag and shake to coat. Dip chicken pieces in egg mixture and shake in bag to coat a second time.

Heat ½ to 1 inch oil in heavy deep skillet on medium-high heat. Brown chicken on all sides. Reduce heat to medium-low and continue cooking until chicken is tender. Do not cover. Turn chicken several times during cooking. Drain on paper towels.

Chicken Jambalaya

6 chicken thighs
½ lb smoked sausage, sliced
1 green pepper, sliced
5 stalks celery, chopped
3 onions, roughly chopped
2 cloves garlic, finely chopped
¼ cup vegetable oil
2 cups regular white rice, uncooked
2½ cups water
1 12-oz can beer
1½ tsp dried rosemary
1 tsp dried thyme
Flour to coat chicken

Chopped parsley
    to taste
Cayenne pepper to
    taste
Salt to taste

Wash the chicken, dry, and coat both sides with cayenne until very red. Let sit for 15 minutes. Heat the oil in the bottom of a large cast iron or aluminum pot. Place the flour and seasonings in a paper bag and shake to mix. Place a few pieces of chicken at a time into the bag and shake to coat. Fry the chicken in the oil until golden brown and remove. Place the sausage, onions, celery, garlic and green pepper into the pot (add more oil if necessary) and sauté until the onions are transparent. Add the herbs and cook for a minute or two, scraping the bottom of the pot to mix. Place the chicken, and a little water into the pot and mix well with the vegetables. Simmer covered over low heat about 30 minutes until chicken is tender. Stir frequently to break up chicken and keep from burning. When the chicken is cooked, wash the rice and stir it into the pot. Pour the warm beer and the remaining water into the pot and continue stirring. Taste and adjust salt and seasonings if necessary. Cover the pot, and keeping the heat low, continue cooking until rice is tender, from 30 to 50 minutes, stirring several times.

Lou's Chicken with Biscuits

2 cups cubed cooked chicken,
10 oz cooked broccoli (1 package frozen)
1 8-oz can cream of chicken soup
¼ cup chopped onion
½ cup sour cream
½ cup grated Cheddar cheese
1½ tsp Worcestershire sauce
Dash curry powder
1 8-oz package refrigerated biscuits
1 egg
1 tsp ground celery seed
½ tsp salt

Preheat oven to 375°. Combine chicken, broccoli, onion, Worcestershire sauce, soup, curry powder, and half the sour cream in a 1½ quart casserole. Mix well. Bake for 20-25 minutes until hot and bubbly. Sprinkle casserole with cheese. Cut biscuits in halves and arrange on top. Mix remaining sour cream, egg, celery seed, and salt and sprinkle over casserole. Return to oven and bake 25 minutes or until golden brown.

Bourbon Chicken

4 chicken breast halves, skinned and boned
¼ cup dark brown sugar
¼ cup Dijon-style mustard
¼ cup bourbon
2 scallions, thinly sliced
1 tsp salt
1 tsp Worcestershire sauce
1 Tbsp margarine
1 Tbsp vegetable oil

Place chicken between 2 sheets of waxed paper and pound to 1/4-inch thickness. Place chicken in a shallow baking dish. Combine sugar, mustard, bourbon, scallions, salt and Worcestershire sauce, and stir well. Brush mixture over both sides of chicken breasts, cover and marinate 1 hour in refrigerator. Remove chicken and reserve marinade.

Combine margarine and oil in large skillet and place over medium-high heat. Sauté chicken 3 to 4 minutes on each side or until done. Remove chicken to a serving platter, and keep warm. Drain and discard pan drippings. Add reserved marinade to skillet, bring to a boil, stirring constantly. Pour sauce over chicken.

Frankie's Spicy Fish Fillets

1½ lbs white fish fillet (cod, flounder, scrod)
¾ cup bread crumbs
1 tsp garlic powder
¼ tsp black pepper
4 Tbsp grated Romano cheese
2 Tbsp chopped fresh parsley
1 tsp ground coriander
½ tsp red pepper flakes
½ tsp dried basil

½ cup flour
1 egg beaten
Hot sauce to taste
Salt to taste
Oil for frying

Place fish fillets in a shallow baking pan. Cover with hot sauce. Marinate in refrigerator approximately 4 hours. Using three separate bowls, put the egg in one, the flour in another, and in the third bowl mix the bread crumbs, herbs, spices, and cheese. Dredge fish fillets first in the flour, next in the egg, and then in the bread crumbs. Press firmly to help bread crumbs adhere to fish.

Pour oil to thinly coat the bottom of a skillet. Heat the oil and add the fish fillets. Cook until browned on both sides. Drain on paper towels and serve.

Creole Fish Fry

1 lb white fish fillet (cod, flounder, scrod)
1 cup milk
2 Tbsp hot Dijon-style mustard
1 Tbsp Creole spices
1 cup cornmeal
Oil for deep frying

Mix milk and mustard. In a separate bowl, mix Creole spices and cornmeal. Dip the fish in the milk-mustard mixture and then cornmeal. Heat a skillet with oil. Fry fish until flaky.

Soaked Shrimp

1–2 lbs raw shrimp, unpeeled
1 Tbsp dried rosemary
2 tsp dried thyme
1 tsp black pepper
2 cloves garlic, peeled and chopped

In a large bowl, combine beer with pancake mix. Heat oil in deep skillet to medium-high temperature. Dip shrimp into beer batter and then drop into oil. Cook until golden brown. Remove cooked shrimp and drain on paper towel to absorb excess oil.

Seafood Rolls

Soft rolls for stuffing
1 stick butter
1 cup chopped onion
½ cup chopped celery
½ cup chopped green pepper
1 cup chopped mushrooms
3 Tbsp flour
½ lb crawfish
¼ lb shrimp
1 lb lump crabmeat
1 pt heavy cream
1 lb Monterey Jack jalapeño cheese, shredded
¼ cup chopped scallions
¼ chopped fresh parsley
1 tsp salt
½ tsp cayenne pepper
½ tsp black pepper
½ tsp garlic powder
1 cup cooked wild rice

Sauté onions, celery, green pepper, and mushrooms in butter and cook until wilted. Add flour and continue cooking for 10 minutes. Add crawfish and shrimp and cook about 7 minutes, stirring occasionally. Blend in heavy cream and jalapeño cheese. When cheese melts, add lump crabmeat, scallions, parsley and seasonings. Remove from heat and add wild rice. Stuff seafood into rolls for serving.

½ tsp dried fennel seed
1 tsp dried celery seed
½ tsp crushed red pepper
8 cups canned clam broth
3 oz tomato paste
1 stick butter
French bread

Roughly grind together rosemary, thyme, and fennel seed. Mix with all other ingredients except shrimp in a large pot and simmer, covered, 1 to 2 hours. Just before serving, add shrimp. Simmer about 2 minutes, stirring, until shrimp are done.

Serve shrimp in bowls with some of the broth. Eat with your fingers and use French bread to soak up the broth.

Brewery Shrimp

1 lb shrimp, shelled and deveined
1 12-oz can warm beer
2½ cups pancake mix
Oil for deep frying

"Knuckleheads have more fun."

— Brenda "The Babe" Frank

Linguine with Shrimp Sauce

1 16-ounce package linguine
½ lb peeled and deveined shrimp
2 Tbsp olive oil
1 28-oz can crushed tomatoes
2 cloves garlic, chopped
1 medium onion, thinly sliced
1 tsp dried oregano
½ tsp crushed red pepper
Freshly ground pepper

Heat olive oil in saucepan. When hot, add garlic, onions, and crushed tomatoes and simmer on low heat until reduced. Cover and simmer for 15 minutes, stirring occasionally. Add oregano and red pepper, cover and simmer for another 5 minutes. Add the shrimp and simmer for 5-7 minutes, until the shrimp are fully cooked. Add freshly ground pepper to taste.

Cook the linguine according to directions and drain. Put the linguine into a serving bowl and pour the sauce over the linguine to serve.

Cajun Crawfish Stew

1½ lbs crawfish tail meat
1 stick butter
½ cup flour
2 onions, chopped fine
2 green peppers, chopped fine
1 stalk celery, chopped fine
2 Tbsp chopped garlic
1 Tbsp salt
¾ Tbsp black pepper
¾ Tbsp cayenne pepper
¾ Tbsp white pepper
¾ Tbsp Creole spice mix
2 cups fish stock (if not available, substitute chicken stock)
1 cup chopped scallions

Melt butter in a large deep skillet. Add flour. Over medium heat stir together and let cook until the color of the roux becomes a deep mahogany. Add the spices, garlic, onions, peppers, and celery until cooked through. Gradually add the heated fish stock, a little at a time, until sauce is the desired thickness. Finish by adding the crawfish tails and cook until done. Garnish with scallions.

Barbecued Shrimp

2 lbs medium-size raw shrimp, peeled and deveined
1 8-oz can tomato sauce
½ cup light molasses
1 tsp mustard powder
Dash hot pepper seasoning sauce
1 clove garlic, minced
1 Tbsp vegetable oil
⅛ tsp dried thyme
Pepper to taste

In a large bowl, mix tomato sauce, molasses, mustard powder, hot pepper, garlic, oil and thyme. Add pepper to taste. Add shrimp and stir to coat. Cover and refrigerate for 4 hours.

Remove shrimp and reserve marinade. Thread skewers with shrimp and place on a lightly oiled grill (or broil on baking sheet about 6 inches below heat). Cook, turning, and brushing often with marinade. When shrimp are opaque in center, about 4 minutes, they are finished. This can also be served as an appetizer.

Blackened Catfish

4 catfish fillets
Olive oil
¼ cup bacon drippings
2 tsp garlic powder
2 tsp dried thyme
2 tsp white pepper
2 tsp black pepper
2 tsp cayenne pepper
2 tsp lemon pepper
2 tsp chili powder
2 tsp rosemary, crushed
2 tsp fennel seed, crushed
Dash allspice
1 tsp oregano
½ tsp salt
¼ cup melted butter
1 Tbsp lemon juice
½ tsp hot sauce
4 scallions, sliced

Heat bacon drippings but do not allow to smoke. Combine all dry ingredients. Rub catfish fillets with olive oil, then coat liberally with spices. Drop in hot fat and cook until

you can put a fork through them. They should be opaque. Be careful not to overcook.

Melt butter and whisk in lemon juice, hot sauce, and scallions. Serve with catfish.

Grilled Shrimp

2 lbs large or jumbo raw shrimp, peeled and deveined
⅓ cup olive oil
¼ cup crushed tomatoes
2 Tbsp red wine vinegar
2 Tbsp chopped fresh basil or 1 tsp dried basil
½ tsp salt
¼ tsp cayenne pepper (or to taste)

In a bowl, stir together the oil, tomatoes, vinegar, basil, and spices. Add the shrimp and toss to coat evenly. Cover and refrigerate two hours, stirring occasionally. Put shrimp on skewers with vegetables of your choice. Cook on medium-hot grill for about 6 minutes, basting with leftover marinade.

"For a great ride, hook a fishtail muffler." "Fishy" Wilson

Macaroni & Cheese

1 8-ounce elbow macaroni
1½ cups milk
1½ tsp powdered mustard
1 tsp Worcestershire sauce
¼ tsp salt
Hot pepper sauce to taste
3½ Tbsp butter
1 egg, beaten
4 cups grated sharp Cheddar cheese
½ cup fresh bread crumbs
½ tsp paprika

Preheat oven to 350°. Butter a shallow, 2-quart baking dish. Cook the macaroni in a large pot of boiling salted water about 8 minutes, until tender but firm. Drain well. In a heavy saucepan, simmer the milk over moderate heat. Remove from the heat and stir in powdered mustard, Worcestershire sauce, salt and hot sauce. Set aside.

In a medium bowl, mix the macaroni with egg and 2 Tbsp of the butter and mix well. Stir in 3 cups Cheddar cheese. Spread the macaroni evenly in the buttered baking dish. Pour the seasoned milk over the macaroni and sprinkle with the remaining cheese. In a small skillet, melt the remaining butter and stir in the bread crumbs until well moistened. Scatter the buttered crumbs evenly over the macaroni and sprinkle with paprika. Bake for 30 minutes, or until the macaroni is bubbling and lightly colored. Transfer baking dish to broiler about 6 inches under heat and cook 2 minutes until bread crumbs are golden brown.

Spaghetti & Meat Sauce

1 16-ounce package spaghetti
1½ lbs ground beef
1 onion, diced
2-3 cloves garlic, crushed
1 28-oz can crushed peeled tomatoes
1 12-oz can tomato paste
1 16-oz can tomato sauce
2-3 cups hot water
1 Tbsp Italian seasoning
1 tsp dried oregano
½ tsp dried basil
¼ tsp crushed red pepper
Black pepper to taste
1 tsp salt

Brown the beef, onion, and garlic in a small skillet. Drain fat and set aside. In a large pot, combine remaining ingredients and allow to simmer for about 15 to 20 minutes. Add beef mixture to sauce and simmer another 1–2 hours.

"Bikers make better lovers."

— "Hogman" Pete

Last Gasp Lasagna

1 lb ground beef
2 Tbsp olive oil
1 16-oz can crushed peeled tomatoes
1 6-oz can tomato paste
1 8-oz can tomato sauce
1 16-oz package lasagna, uncooked
2 cups shredded mozzarella cheese
4 cups ricotta cheese
3 Tbsp grated Parmesan cheese

In a saucepan, brown beef in oil. Drain. Add tomatoes, tomato paste, and sauce, and simmer 15 minutes, stirring occasionally. Cook lasagna according to package directions; drain.

Preheat oven to 375°. Spread ½ cup meat sauce on bottom of 9 x 13 baking dish. Place 4 pasta pieces over sauce to cover. Spread ⅓ each of mozzarella and ricotta cheeses over pasta. Cover with ½ remaining sauce. Repeat layers twice, beginning and ending with pasta, and spread remaining sauce on top. Sprinkle the top with Parmesan cheese. Cover with foil. Bake for 30 minutes or until hot and bubbly. Remove foil and bake 5 minutes more. Let stand 5–10 minutes before cutting.

Total Pizza

1 package prepared pizza dough
1 onion, thinly sliced
1 sweet red pepper, seeded and sliced into strips
1 green pepper, seeded and sliced into strips
½ cup sliced mushrooms
3 Tbsp olive oil
½ lb sweet Italian sausage
½ lb sliced pepperoni
3 oz goat cheese
10 oz mozzarella cheese, coarsely grated
2 Tbsp freshly grated Parmesan cheese
2 cups tomato sauce

Preheat oven to 425°. Prepare pizza dough according to instructions and prebake in 1 Tbsp oil for about 5 minutes.

Sauté onions, peppers, and mushrooms in remaining olive oil over medium heat, stirring frequently, until peppers are soft. Set aside. Brown sausage, breaking into pieces, and drain off excess fat. Chop sausage coarsely and set aside. Spread tomato sauce over pizza, crumble goat cheese on top. Add onions, mushrooms, peppers, sausage, pepperoni, and remaining cheeses. Bake 10 minutes or until crust is slightly brown and cheese is bubbly.

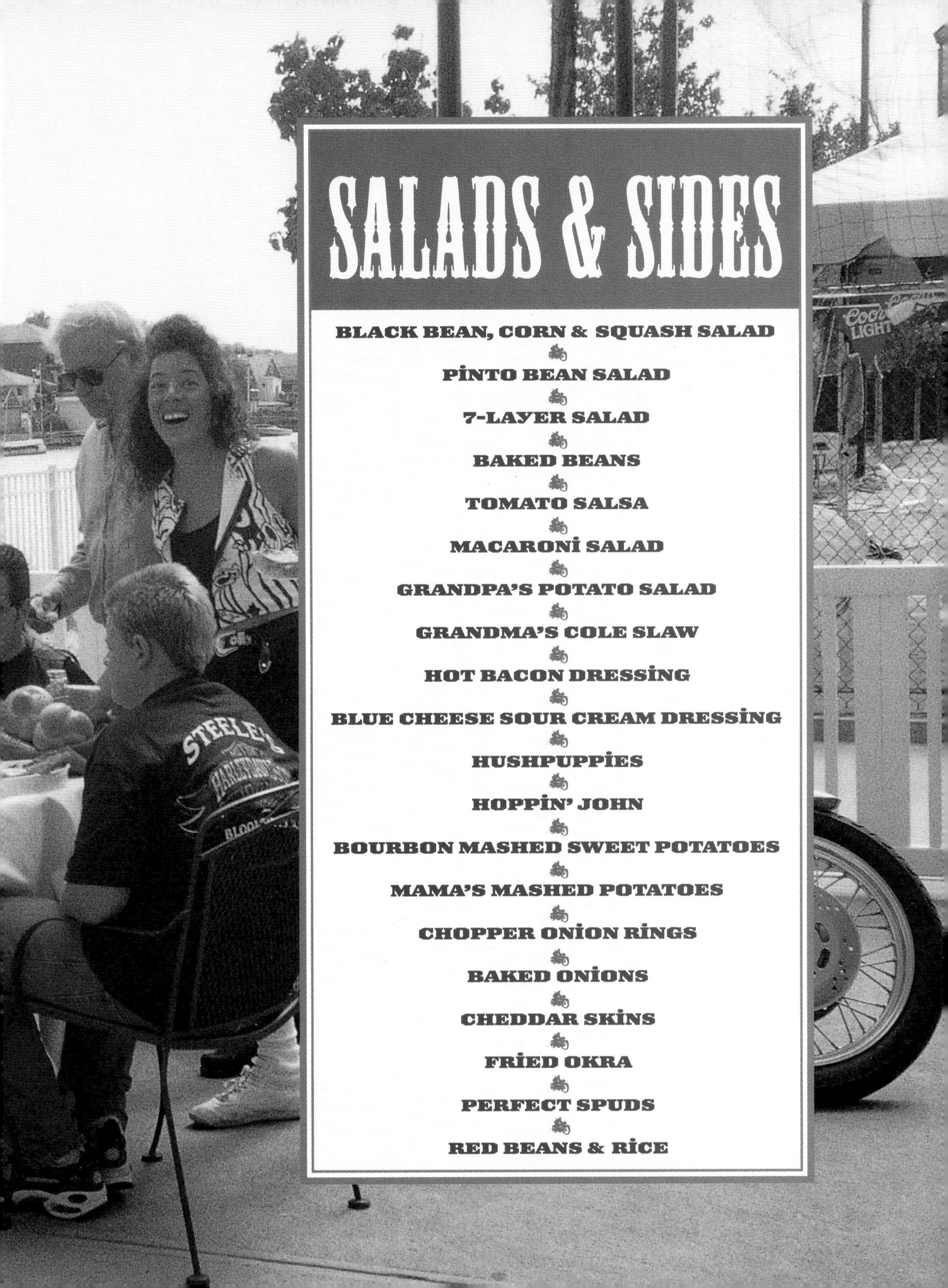

SALADS & SIDES

BLACK BEAN, CORN & SQUASH SALAD

PINTO BEAN SALAD

7-LAYER SALAD

BAKED BEANS

TOMATO SALSA

MACARONI SALAD

GRANDPA'S POTATO SALAD

GRANDMA'S COLE SLAW

HOT BACON DRESSING

BLUE CHEESE SOUR CREAM DRESSING

HUSHPUPPIES

HOPPIN' JOHN

BOURBON MASHED SWEET POTATOES

MAMA'S MASHED POTATOES

CHOPPER ONION RINGS

BAKED ONIONS

CHEDDAR SKINS

FRIED OKRA

PERFECT SPUDS

RED BEANS & RICE

Black Bean, Corn & Squash Salad

1⅓ cups dried black beans, rinsed, and soaked overnight in water
3 ears corn or 1½ cups canned corn
1 cup chopped red onion
1 red pepper, chopped
½ cup chopped Italian parsley
¼ cup chopped fresh cilantro
¼ cup white wine vinegar
1 Tbsp lemon juice
½ cup olive oil
¼ tsp cumin
1 lb mixture of summer squash and zucchini, cut into ½-inch rounds
3 cloves garlic, chopped

Drain black beans and place in a heavy saucepan with enough fresh cold water to cover beans. Bring to a boil. Reduce heat to medium and simmer until beans are tender, stirring occasionally, for about 1½ hours. Drain well. Transfer to large bowl and cool.

Cook corn in pot of boiling water until tender, but not overdone. Drain, cool, and cut corn kernels off cobs, or if using canned corn, drain and set aside. Heat a small amount of oil in frying pan over medium heat. Sauté squash and garlic together until cooked *al dente*. Remove from heat. To cooled beans, add corn, squash, onion, pepper, parsley, and cilantro. In a small bowl, whisk vinegar and lemon juice together. Add cumin. Gradually whisk in oil. Pour dressing over salad and toss well. Season with salt and pepper and serve at room temperature.

Pinto Bean Salad

1½ cups dried pinto beans, soaked overnight and drained
2 Tbsp salt
1 bay leaf
3 medium tomatoes, chopped
1 medium red onion, thinly sliced
2 scallions, sliced
3 Tbsp fresh lemon juice
1 Tbsp fresh lime juice
1 tsp salt
½ cup olive oil
3 large garlic cloves, minced
¼ cup fresh cilantro, chopped
Salt and pepper to taste

Put the pinto beans in a large pot and cover with fresh water. Add the bay leaf and bring to a boil. Reduce heat and simmer the beans for 30 minutes. Stir in the salt and simmer another 30 minutes until beans are tender. Remove the bay leaf and discard. Drain the beans and allow to cool until warm.

Combine the lemon and lime juice. Beat in the olive oil gradually until well mixed. Add the garlic and cilantro. Check seasonings and add salt and pepper if desired. Pour dressing over warm beans and mix until well coated. Add the chopped tomatoes and onions and toss well.

7-Layer Salad

1 small head iceberg lettuce
½ cup finely chopped onion
½ cup finely chopped celery
1 4-oz can water chestnuts, thinly sliced
2 packages frozen peas
2 cups mayonnaise
½ cup grated Parmesan cheese
2 Tbsp sugar
1 lb bacon, cooked and chopped
   (or ¾ jar bacon bits)
6 hard-boiled eggs, chopped
Salt and pepper to taste

Place first 5 ingredients in a bowl in the order listed. Cover with mayonnaise. Sprinkle with grated Parmesan cheese and sugar. Cover tightly with foil. Let sit at least 8 hours in refrigerator. Crumble cooked bacon over top. Cover with fine chopped eggs, season with salt and pepper.

Baked Beans

1 lb navy or pea beans, soaked in water
   overnight and drained
½ lb salt pork or slab bacon, cut
   into ½-inch pieces
1 cup chopped onion
3 cloves garlic, chopped
⅓ cup dark molasses
1 cup brown sugar
1 cup ketchup
1 tsp mustard powder
¼ tsp pepper
½ tsp salt

Rinse beans and place in a large pot or saucepan with a good amount of cold fresh water to cover. Bring to a boil, reduce heat, and simmer until tender, approximately 1 hour. Reserve liquid.
   Preheat oven to 300°. In a large casserole or Dutch oven, sauté pork or bacon until crispy. Add onions and garlic and cook until translucent. Add molasses, sugar, ketchup, mustard powder, salt and pepper and mix well. Add the drained beans. Cover and bake in 300° oven for approximately 2 hours. Stir occasionally and add reserved liquid if needed.

Tomato Salsa

3 medium tomatoes, peeled and finely
   chopped
2 hot chile peppers, peeled, seeded and
   finely chopped, or 1 4-oz can chopped
   chile peppers
½ cup finely chopped onion
2 large garlic cloves, minced
¼ cup chopped fresh cilantro
1 tsp lime juice
Salt and pepper to taste

Combine all ingredients. Add additional vegetables if desired. Ingredients may be prepared in a food processor but should not be pureed. Refrigerate for several hours or overnight. Best served at room temperature.

Macaroni Salad

8-oz package elbow macaroni, cooked
   and drained
1 cup chopped celery
½ cup chopped green pepper
½ cup chopped red pepper
⅓ cup chopped onion
½ cup chopped Cheddar cheese
¾ cup mayonnaise
2 Tbsp apple cider vinegar
1 Tbsp prepared mustard
1 tsp sugar
1 tsp salt
½ tsp ground pepper

Mix the macaroni, celery, pepper, onion, and Cheddar cheese in a large bowl. Whisk together the mayonnaise, vinegar, mustard, sugar, salt and pepper until smooth. Pour dressing over the macaroni and vegetables, mix well, and refrigerate.

Grandpa's Potato Salad

12 large new potatoes
½ tsp salt
8 eggs, hard-boiled and chopped
1 cup mayonnaise
½ cup prepared yellow mustard
3 Tbsp apple cider vinegar
2 large onions, chopped
1 large jar chopped pimentos
2 large stalks celery, chopped
1 tsp dried celery seed
1 jar of sweet pickles, finely chopped

In a large pot, cover the potatoes with water and add the salt. Boil until potatoes are tender when pierced with a fork, but do not overcook. Chop the potatoes into cubes.

Put the chopped potatoes, eggs, onions,

pimentos, sweet pickles, celery, and celery seed in a large bowl. In a small bowl, mix together mayonnaise, mustard and vinegar, and stir until smooth. Pour mixture over the chopped vegetables and gently fold to coat. Chill several hours or overnight before serving.

Grandma's Cole Slaw

1 small head cabbage, shredded
2 carrots, peeled and shredded
1 small white onion, grated
½ cup buttermilk
½ cup mayonnaise
3 Tbsp apple cider vinegar
1 Tbsp sugar
1 tsp salt
½ tsp freshly ground black pepper
¼ tsp white pepper
1 small Granny Smith apple, grated

Mix the cabbage, carrots, and onion in a large bowl. Whisk together the remaining ingredients minus the apple, to make a smooth dressing. Add grated apple to dressing. Refrigerate. About 30 minutes before serving, mix the dressing with the

Hot Bacon Dressing

½ lb bacon, diced
1 small onion, minced
3 eggs, beaten
2 Tbsp flour
1 Tbsp mustard powder
2 Tbsp sugar
½ cup cider vinegar
1 tsp Worcestershire
   sauce
1 Tbsp dried dill
Salt and pepper to taste

Sauté bacon and onion until bacon is browned and onion is translucent. Remove bacon and onions and set aside, but leave bacon drippings in pan. In a bowl, beat together eggs, flour, mustard powder, sugar, vinegar, Worcestershire and dill. Stir egg mixture into hot bacon drippings and cook over low heat, stirring until thick, approximately 3–5 minutes. Season with salt and pepper.

Blue Cheese Sour Cream Dressing

½ cup mayonnaise
½ cup sour cream
1 cup crumbled
   blue cheese
½ cup buttermilk
Salt and pepper to taste

Place mayonnaise and sour cream in

container; fold in blue cheese. Gradually stir in small amounts of buttermilk until dressing reaches desired consistency. Season to taste with salt and pepper. Cover container and refrigerate overnight. Keeps for a few days.

Hushpuppies

1 cup cornmeal
1 cup flour
1 medium onion, minced
2 tsp baking powder
1 tsp salt
½ tsp black pepper
1 egg beaten
¼ tsp hot sauce
¾ cup buttermilk
3 cups vegetable oil

Mix dry ingredients and onion together. Mix in the egg, hot sauce, and buttermilk. Let thick batter sit for 1/2 hour.

Heat oil in deep dryer. Drop batter into pan by teaspoons. Fry until golden brown. Drain on paper towels and serve immediately. Can be served with ketchup, butter, malt vinegar, or honey.

Hoppin' John

1 cup dried black-eyed peas, rinsed
   and drained
¼ lb bacon
4 cups boiling water
1 tsp salt
1 tsp chili powder
¼ tsp hot sauce
½ cup chopped onion
2 cups cooked rice
Salt and pepper to taste

Cook peas with bacon in boiling water until peas are almost tender. Add seasonings and

onion. Continue to cook until peas are done and most liquid is absorbed. Add rice and heat through. Add pepper and more salt if needed.

Bourbon Mashed Sweet Potatoes

6 sweet potatoes (about 2 lbs)
¼ cup heavy cream
2 Tbsp bourbon
2 Tbsp maple syrup
2 Tbsp butter
Salt and pepper to taste

Roast potatoes in skins in a 425° oven for 40 minutes. Remove the skin from the sweet potatoes and discard. Place sweet potatoes in a large sauce pan. Over low heat, partially mash, then add the cream, bourbon, maple syrup and butter. Continue to mash until all the ingredients are mixed and the potatoes are smooth but there are a few small lumps. Add more butter if needed. Season with salt and pepper.

Mama's Mashed Potatoes

8–10 small, all-purpose potatoes, peeled and cut into 2-inch cubes
1 stalk celery, including leaves, whole
1 bay leaf
1 large clove garlic, whole
4 Tbsp butter, chopped into small pieces.
¼ cup heavy cream
¼ cup milk
½ cup grated Parmesan cheese
½ tsp salt
Fresh pepper to taste

Place peeled potatoes in a large cooking pot. Add enough cold water to cover potatoes. Add celery, bay leaf, and garlic. Bring to a boil and simmer, covered, for 20 to 30 minutes, or until potatoes are tender. Pour off cooking liquid. Discard the bay leaf, celery, and garlic. To the potatoes in the pan, add butter, cheese, half the cream, half the milk, and fresh pepper. Mash by hand or with an electric mixer. Use additional cream and milk until potatoes reach desired consistency.

Chopper Onion Rings

1 large Spanish onion
1 cup flour, sifted
2 tsp salt
1 tsp pepper
1 tsp paprika
1½ tsp baking powder
1 egg, separated
⅔ cup milk
1 Tbsp salad oil
Oil for frying

Peel onion and slice into separate rings, about ¼ inch thick. Cover with cold water and let stand for 30 minutes. Drain and spread out on paper towels. Sift flour, salt, pepper, paprika, and baking powder in bowl and set aside. Beat egg yolk slightly, stir in milk and tablespoon salad oil. Add this to flour mixture and stir until smooth.

Beat egg white until stiff peaks form. Fold into batter. Heat about 1 inch of oil in medium-hot skillet. Dip onion rings in batter and let excess batter drip off. Drop several rings at a time into hot fat and fry until golden. Drain on paper towel.

Baked Onions

4 lbs large, sweet onions, such as Vidalia
3 cloves garlic, minced
1 stick butter, melted
1 10-oz can cream of mushroom soup
1 cup half and half
¼ tsp salt
¼ tsp black pepper
1 cup grated sharp Cheddar cheese
¼ cup grated Parmesan cheese
8 slices French bread, about 3/4 inch thick
3 Tbsp butter, melted

Preheat oven to 350°. Slice onion, and cut each slice in half. Sauté onion slices and garlic in butter in a large skillet until barely translucent. Transfer onions to a lightly greased 9 x 13-inch baking dish.

Combine soup, half and half, salt and pepper and pour mixture over onions. Sprinkle cheeses evenly over sauce.

Arrange bread slices on top and brush with 3 tablespoons butter. Bake for 35 minutes or until golden brown.

Cheddar Skins

2 baking potatoes
4 slices lean bacon, cooked and diced
1 cup shredded Cheddar cheese
Sour cream (optional)

Preheat the oven to 400°. Wash and wrap the potatoes in aluminum foil. Pierce each potato with a fork and bake for 1 hour. Remove the foil from the potatoes and cut them in half lengthwise. With a spoon, scoop out ¼ to ½ of each potato. Use the potato insides in another recipe.

Sprinkle the cheese evenly over the potatoes. Add the bacon. Bake until the cheese melts. Serve with sour cream if desired.

Fried Okra

1 lb okra
½ tsp salt
¼ tsp pepper
1½ cups buttermilk
2 cups self-rising cornmeal
Vegetable oil

Wash okra and drain well. Remove tip and steam end and cut into ½-inch slices. Sprinkle okra with salt. Add buttermilk, stirring until well coated. Let stand at least 15 minutes, then drain okra well. Dredge in cornmeal. Deep fry okra in hot oil until golden brown. Drain on paper towels.

Perfect Spuds

6 large baking potatoes
Vegetable oil to coat
Rock salt
1 stick butter
½ cup sour cream

Wash potatoes thoroughly and dry. Apply thin coating of vegetable oil to potato

skins. Preheat oven to 425°. Pour enough rock salt into baking pan to cover the bottom. Place the potatoes on top of the salt layer with a bit of space between them. Cover the potatoes completely with rock salt, filling in gaps between potatoes. Bake for 1 hour.

Remove from oven. Carefully brush aside top salt later and lift each potato out with fork or tongs. Brush away any salt that may have stuck to the potato skin. Slice each in half and serve with butter, sour cream, and any other topping.

Red Beans & Rice

1 lb red beans, soaked overnight
1 medium onion, chopped
1 bunch scallions, chopped
¼ cup chopped garlic
½ cup fresh parsley
1 stalk celery, chopped
½ cup ketchup
1 green pepper, seeded and chopped
1 Tbsp Worcestershire sauce
2 Tbsp hot sauce
1 tsp dried thyme
½ tsp ground sage
Pinch cayenne pepper
Salt and pepper to taste
1 lb smoked sausage, cut into 1-inch pieces
1 ham shank
4 cups cooked rice (approx.)

Drain beans. Place beans in a large pot and cover with fresh, cold water. Cover and cook for 1 hour or until beans are tender. Add all remaining ingredients except salt and rice. Bring to a boil over medium heat. Reduce heat and simmer until beans are tender, about 2½ hours. Remove ham shank. Remove about ¼ cup beans and, in a small bowl, mash to a paste. Return bean paste to mixture and stir. Simmer 15 more minutes and serve over rice.

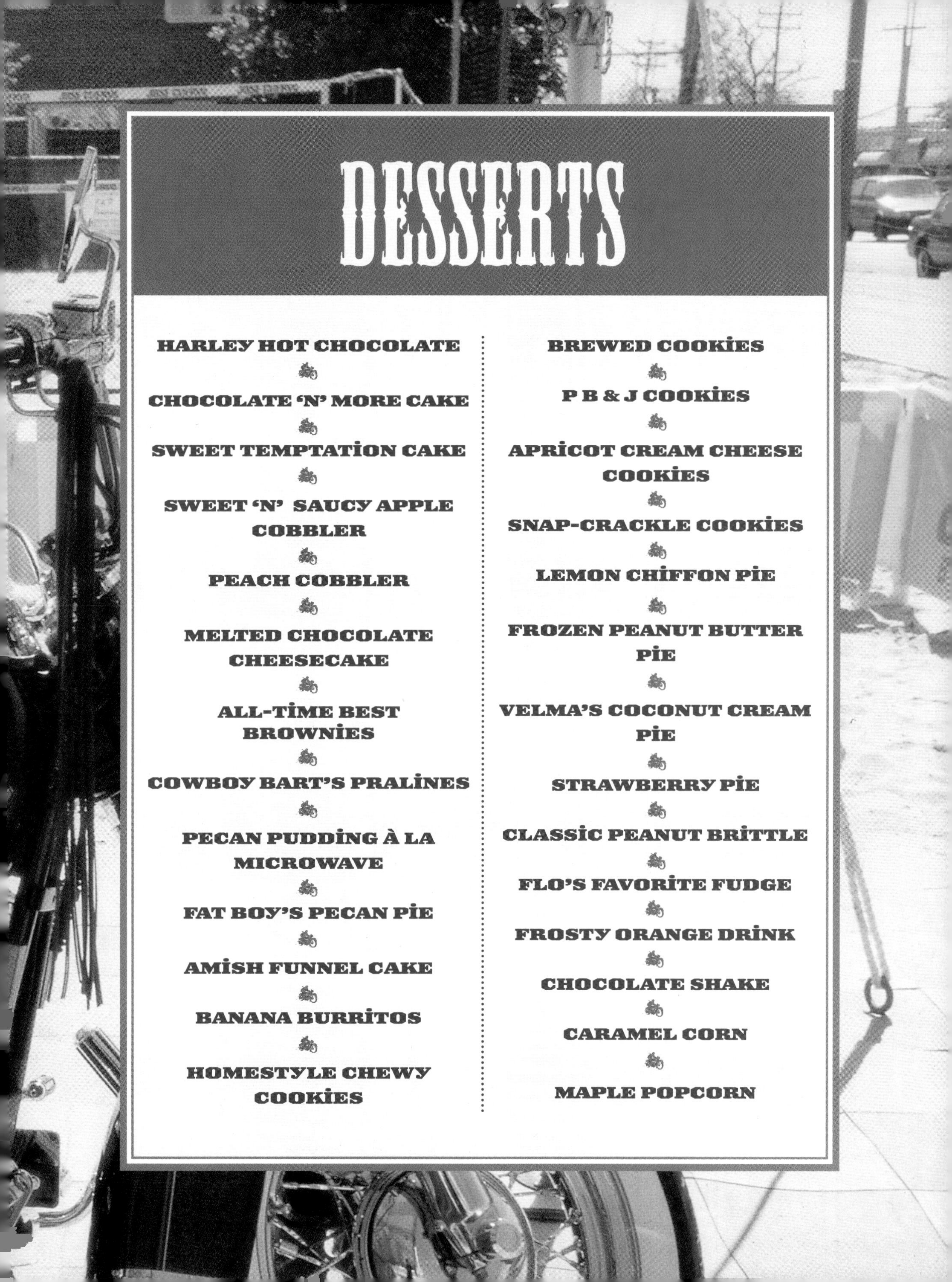

DESSERTS

HARLEY HOT CHOCOLATE

CHOCOLATE 'N' MORE CAKE

SWEET TEMPTATION CAKE

SWEET 'N' SAUCY APPLE COBBLER

PEACH COBBLER

MELTED CHOCOLATE CHEESECAKE

ALL-TIME BEST BROWNIES

COWBOY BART'S PRALINES

PECAN PUDDING À LA MICROWAVE

FAT BOY'S PECAN PIE

AMISH FUNNEL CAKE

BANANA BURRITOS

HOMESTYLE CHEWY COOKIES

BREWED COOKIES

P B & J COOKIES

APRICOT CREAM CHEESE COOKIES

SNAP-CRACKLE COOKIES

LEMON CHIFFON PIE

FROZEN PEANUT BUTTER PIE

VELMA'S COCONUT CREAM PIE

STRAWBERRY PIE

CLASSIC PEANUT BRITTLE

FLO'S FAVORITE FUDGE

FROSTY ORANGE DRINK

CHOCOLATE SHAKE

CARAMEL CORN

MAPLE POPCORN

NOTE: In any recipe calling for flour, use pre-sifted all-purpose flour unless otherwise indicated. In recipes calling for brown sugar, use either light or dark brown sugar, according to taste preference. Dark brown sugar is more intense.

Harley Hot Chocolate

1 cup heavy cream
2-oz unsweetened chocolate, broken into pieces
2-oz semi-sweet chocolate, broken into pieces
¼ cup granulated sugar
½ tsp vanilla extract
3 cups whole milk
Marshmallows (optional)
Whipped cream (optional)
Cinnamon (optional)

In a saucepan, heat the heavy cream to scalding until tiny bubbles form around the edge of the pan. Remove from heat and stir in chocolate pieces until they melt and mixture is smooth. Add the sugar and vanilla and stir until smooth. Pour in the milk. Return the saucepan to the stove and heat on medium until the mixture is hot and steaming. Do not bring to a boil. Top with marshmallows or whipped cream and sprinkle with cinnamon if desired.

Chocolate 'n' More Cake

Nonstick spray
Flour for dusting pan
¼ lb unsalted butter
3 1½-oz chocolate bars, broken up
⅔ cup granulated sugar
3 eggs
1 tsp vanilla extract
2 cups graham cracker crumbs
1½ cups mini marshmallows

Preheat oven to 350°. Spray the bottom and sides of an 8-inch cake pan with nonstick spray, line the bottom with waxed paper, spray with more shortening, and dust with the flour. In a large heavy saucepan, melt the butter over medium heat. When the butter is halfway melted, add the chocolate and stir until most is melted. Remove from heat and stir until both are fully melted. Add remaining ingredients and pour into the pan. Bake for 30 minutes, or until the top is brown and the edges are crusty. Cool in the pan for 20 minutes. Run a knife around the edges of the cake, cover with waxed paper, and invert onto a plate. Remove the pan and peel off the paper. Invert again and cool about 15 minutes more.

Sweet Temptation Cake

1 lb butter, softened
3 cups granulated sugar
6 eggs
3½ cups flour
1 cup cocoa powder
1 cup plain yogurt
2 tsp vanilla extract
2 tsp baking powder

Preheat oven to 350°. Cream butter and sugar. Add eggs and beat well. Mix baking powder with 2 cups flour, add to batter and continue to beat. Add yogurt, vanilla, and remaining flour and mix well. Butter 10-inch Bundt pan and dust with cocoa powder. Pour batter into pan. Bake about 1 hour or until cake pulls away from edges of pan. Cool in pan for 20 minutes before removing.

Sweet 'n' Saucy Apple Cobbler

1 stick butter
3 lb baking apples, peeled, cored, and sliced
2 Tbsp fresh lemon juice
½ cup granulated sugar
1½ Tbsp flour
1 tsp vanilla extract

Crust:
2 cups flour
¼ cup sugar
2 tsp baking powder
¼ tsp salt
2 Tbsp butter, chilled and cut into small cubes
⅓ cup coarsely chopped crystallized ginger
Zest of 1 orange
1 cup heavy cream

Preheat oven to 450°. Melt butter in saut pan over medium heat. Stir in apples, lemon juice, sugar, and flour. Cover partially and cook until tender, about 15 minutes. Stir in vanilla. Transfer mixture to buttered 10-inch pie dish.

In a bowl, combine flour, sugar, baking powder and salt. Cut in butter with a pastry blender or use your fingertips until mixture is crumbly. Stir in ginger. Stir orange zest into cream, and then, using a fork, stir cream into flour until dough is formed. Knead dough briefly, then roll out to fit pie dish. Place over pie filling and trim excess. Cut a hole in center of crust and brush with cream. Bake 10 minutes. Reduce heat to 375° and bake 20 to 25 minutes more. Serve with whipped cream on top if desired.

Peach Cobbler

4 cups sliced fresh peaches or
   2 bags frozen
¼ cup granulated sugar
1 tsp cinnamon
1 Tbsp fresh lemon juice

Crust:
½ cup butter
1½ cups flour
2 Tbsp baking powder
½ tsp salt
1 cup sugar
1 cup milk

Preheat oven to 350°. In a bowl, mix together the peaches, sugar, cinnamon, and lemon juice. Let stand while preparing batter.

Place butter in 9 x 13 baking dish and put in oven. While butter is melting, mix the bottom crust by combining flour, baking powder, salt, sugar and milk. When the butter is completely melted, remove baking pan and pour in batter. Then spoon peach mixture evenly over the batter. Return dish to oven and bake for 45 minutes.

Melted Chocolate Cheesecake

1 9-oz package chocolate wafer cookies
4 Tbsp butter, melted
3 8-oz pkgs cream cheese, softened
1 cup granulated sugar
4 eggs
1 Tbsp vanilla extract
1 cup heavy cream
1½ lbs snack-size chocolate candy bars
cut into pieces
Heavy cream, whipped, and fudge sauce (optional)

Preheat oven to 325°. In a food processor, grind cookies into fine crumbs. Add butter and process until well blended. Press into the bottom and slightly up the sides of a 10-inch springform pan. In a large bowl, beat together cream cheese and sugar with an electric mixer on medium speed until smooth. Beat in eggs, one at a time. Beat in vanilla and cream. Fold in 1½ cups candy bar pieces. Turn the batter into pan. Bake 1¼ hours, or until cheesecake is almost set but center still jiggles slightly. Let cool to room temperature. Sprinkle remaining candy pieces over top of cheesecake and refrigerate at least 4 to 5 hours before serving. Run a knife around

edge of pan to loosen cake and remove springform side. Can be served with fudge topping and whipped cream.

All-Time Best Brownies

6 Tbsp butter or margarine, softened
⅔ cup granulated sugar
2 large eggs
¼ cup milk
1 tsp vanilla extract
½ cup flour
1 4-oz package regular chocolate pudding mix
½ tsp baking powder
¼ tsp salt
½ cup chopped nuts of choice
Confectioners' sugar (optional)

Preheat oven to 350°. Cream butter and sugar. Blend in eggs, milk, and vanilla. Stir together flour, pudding mix, baking powder, and salt. Add this to butter mixture and mix well. Stir in nuts. Grease a 9 x 9 x 2 baking pan and spread in batter. Bake for 25 to 30 minutes. Cool. Sift confectioners' sugar over top, if desired. Cut into bars. Makes 24.

Cowboy Bart's Pralines

2 cups granulated sugar
1 tsp baking soda
1 cup buttermilk
2 tsp vanilla extract
Dash ground cinnamon
2 cups pecan halves, toasted
    at 300° until done (watch
    out—they burn quickly!)

Combine sugar, baking soda, and buttermilk in heavy saucepan. Cook on medium heat, stirring constantly until mixture forms a soft ball in cold water (240° on a candy thermometer). Remove from heat. Add vanilla and pecans and beat until mixture turns cloudy and pecans do not sink to the bottom of pan.

Working quickly, drop by quarter-cups onto buttered waxed paper. If candy gets too hard before all is spooned out, add a little water and reheat, or let the pan stand over very low heat or in a bowl of hot water while spooning out. Note: Dish towels under the waxed paper will prevent it from melting onto your countertop. Makes 15.

Pecan Pudding à la Microwave

1 Tbsp butter
1 large egg, beaten
    ⅓ cup dark corn syrup
    ¼ tsp vanilla extract
    2 Tbsp flour
    ⅛ tsp baking powder
    ¼ cup chopped pecans
    Confectioners' sugar

In a large microwave-proof dish, microwave butter, uncovered, about 30 seconds or until just melted. Swirl the butter in the dish, coating the entire surface. In a bowl, lightly beat the egg. Pour the excess butter from the dish into the beaten egg. Stir in the corn syrup and vanilla.

Stir together flour and baking powder. Stir flour mixture into egg mixture. Gently fold in the chopped pecans. Pour mixture into buttered custard cup. Microwave, uncovered, on 50% power for 3 to 4 minutes until the mixture is just set. Rotate every minute if necessary. Sift a little confectioners' sugar onto top. Serve warm. Light cream can be poured over pudding if desired.

Fat Boy's Pecan Pie

3 large eggs
⅔ cup granulated sugar
½ tsp salt
½ cup melted butter
1 cup light or dark corn syrup
1 cup pecans
1 unbaked 9-inch pie shell
½ cup semisweet chocolate chips
   (optional)

Preheat oven to 375°. Beat eggs, sugar, and salt. Add butter and syrup. Mix in pecans. Bake in pie shell 40-45 minutes. If adding chocolate chips, mix in with pecans.

Amish Funnel Cake

1 egg
⅔ cup milk
1¼ cups flour
1 tsp baking powder
2 Tbsp granulated sugar
¼ tsp salt
Confectioners' sugar, sifted
Vegetable oil for frying

Beat egg with milk. Blend flour, sugar, baking powder, and salt. Slowly add the egg mixture, beating until smooth. Heat about 1 inch of oil in skillet to medium high. Using a funnel, place index finger over bottom opening and pour in batter. Remove your finger and using a circular motion allow batter to drop into hot oil in spirals. Remove each cake when golden brown. While cake is still warm, sprinkle with confectioners' sugar. Best served warm.

Banana Burritos

2½ lbs bananas, sliced
   ¼-inch thick
2 Tbsp butter
1 cup brown sugar
½ cup granulated sugar
1 tsp nutmeg
   1 Tbsp cinnamon
      2 tsp honey
      ¾ cup rum
         1 egg
         1 Tbsp milk
         2 12-inch flour
      tortillas

Melt butter in sauté pan. Add the sugar, spices, honey, and rum. Let simmer over medium heat for 5 minutes or until mixture reaches consistency of maple syrup. Add sliced bananas to the pan. Cook for 1-1½ minutes or until bananas become slightly soft. Remove pan from heat and pour contents through a strainer. Remove bananas from the strainer and put them into refrigerator to cool. Reserve strained sauce in another container.

After bananas cool, mix together the egg and milk in a bowl. Lay out the tortillas. Place ¼ of banana mixture and sauce on each tortilla, leaving room at the edges. Brush the edges of the tortilla with the egg wash. Fold the sides of the tortilla toward the middle and then roll tortilla closed like a burrito. Heat oil in pan until medium hot and lay burrito in hot oil. Fry until golden brown. Remove and place on a paper towel. Slice diagonally with a serrated knife and serve with the remainder of the sauce. Add ice cream for a special touch.

Homestyle Chewy Cookies

1 cup margarine or butter
¾ cup brown sugar, packed
¾ cup granulated sugar
2 eggs
1¾ cup flour
2 cups old fashioned oatmeal
2 tsp ground cinnamon
1 tsp baking soda
½ tsp salt (optional)
1 Tbsp sugar

Preheat oven to 375°. Grease cookie sheet. In a large bowl, beat together butter, brown sugar, and regular sugar until light and fluffy. Add eggs and mix well. In a medium bowl, combine flour, oats, cinnamon, baking soda, and salt. Add to sugar mixture and blend well. Drop by rounded teaspoonfuls onto prepared cookie sheet. Combine tablespoon sugar and remaining cinnamon and sprinkle lightly over cookies. Bake 8 to 10 minutes. Cool at least 1 minute before removing.

Brewed Cookies

2 cups flour
½ tsp baking soda
½ cup brown sugar
1 tsp cinnamon
½ cup butter
1¼ cups room temperature beer
½ cup chopped walnuts

Preheat oven to 350°. Cream together the butter and brown sugar. Cut in the flour, baking soda, and cinnamon. Slowly blend in the beer to form a soft dough. Drop by teaspoonsful onto baking sheet and top each cookie with a walnut piece. Bake for 12 to 15 minutes until lightly brown. Cool for 1 minute and remove to wire rack. Makes 2–3 dozen.

P B & J Cookies

½ cup shortening
½ cup peanut butter
½ cup granulated sugar
½ cup packed brown sugar
1 egg
1¼ cup flour
¾ tsp baking soda
½ tsp baking powder
¼ tsp salt
Jam or jelly

Preheat oven to 375°. In a mixing bowl, cream together shortening, peanut butter, and sugars. Beat in egg. Combine dry ingredients and gradually

preserves. Bake for 15 minutes. After cookies are cool, sprinkle with confectioners' sugar.

add to creamed mixture. Cover and chill 1 hour.

Roll dough into 1-inch balls and place 2 inches apart on a greased baking sheet. Flatten slightly. Bake for 10 minutes and cool on wire rack. Assemble the cookies by spreading jam or jelly on half the cookies and covering with the remaining cookies to make a sandwich. Makes 4 dozen.

Apricot Cream Cheese Cookies

1½ cups butter or margarine
1½ cups granulated sugar
1 8-oz package cream cheese, softened
2 eggs
2 Tbsp lemon juice
1½ tsp grated lemon peel
4½ cups flour
1½ tsp baking powder
1 cup apricot preserves
Confectioners' sugar

Preheat oven to 350°. Combine butter or margarine with sugar and softened cream cheese until blended. Add the eggs, lemon juice, lemon peel, and mix. Combine the dry ingredients and add to sugar mix, stirring well. Chill dough until stiff.

Shape dough into balls. Place on ungreased cookie sheet and flatten slightly. Push in the centers with back of a spoon or your thumb, and fill with

Snap-Crackle Cookies

½ cup butter or margarine
1 cup granulated sugar
¼ tsp salt
1 egg, beaten
2 cups Rice Krispies©
¾ cup chopped dates or raisins
1 cup chopped pecans

Melt butter in saucepan. Add sugar, salt and egg, and cook until thick. Add dates or raisins and continue cooking about 4 to 5 minutes, stirring constantly. Add Rice Krispies and half the pecans and stir gently to mix. Use teaspoons to form balls and roll balls in remaining pecans. Place balls on waxed paper and cool for 30 minutes. Makes 4 dozen.

Lemon Chiffon Pie

1 Tbsp unflavored gelatin
½ cup cold water
4 eggs, separated
1 cup granulated sugar
½ cup lemon juice
½ tsp salt
1 Tbsp grated lemon rind
Graham cracker pie crust
1 pint whipped cream

Soften gelatin in water for 5 minutes. Beat eggs yolks and add sugar, lemon juice, and salt. Cook mixture over boiling water until consistency is like custard. Add grated lemon rind and softened gelatin and stir thoroughly. Cool. Beat egg whites with remaining 1/2 cup sugar until stiff peaks form. When custard mixture begins to thicken, fold in egg whites. Fill crumb crust with filling and chill. Spread with whipped cream.

Frozen Peanut Butter Pie

1½ cups chocolate wafer crumbs
⅓ cup butter or margarine, melted
1 cup marshmallow cream
½ cup peanut butter (chunky or smooth)
1 3-oz package cream cheese, softened
¼ cup milk
½ cup heavy cream
2 Tbsp granulated sugar
¼ cup peanuts, coarsely chopped (optional)
Chocolate curls for garnish (optional)

In a small bowl, combine chocolate wafer crumbs and melted butter. Press firmly into bottom and a little up the sides of a 9-inch pie plate. Place the marshmallow cream, peanut butter,and cream cheese in a large bowl. With electric mixer, beat until blended. Gradually beat in milk until mixture is smooth. In another bowl., beat heavy cream and sugar until stiff. Gently fold whipped cream into peanut butter mixture.

Spoon filling into chocolate crust. Sprinkle with chopped peanuts. Freeze 3 hours or until firm. Before serving, let stand at room temperature about 10 minutes. Garnish with chocolate curls.

Velma's Coconut Cream Pie

9-oz package vanilla pudding
5-oz whipped topping
4½ cups cold milk
1½ cups packaged coconut
½ cup toasted coconut
2 baked pie shells

To toast coconut: Spread coconut on a baking sheet and place in a 300° oven for approximately 6 to 8 minutes. Check frequently; it will brown quickly.

Mix together pudding, whipped topping, milk and coconut. Pour into baked pie shells and top with toasted coconut. Chill. Makes 2 pies.

Strawberry Pie

1 cup granulated sugar
3 Tbsp cornstarch
1 pt fresh strawberries, cut up
1 12-oz can lemon-lime soda
1 pint whipped cream

Crust:
1 cup flour
¼ tsp salt
¾ stick butter
1½ Tbsp shortening
⅛ cup ice water

In a medium-sized saucepan, combine sugar, cornstarch, and soda. Stir until creamy, then cook over a medium high heat until the mixture becomes thick. Cool to room temperature.

Preheat oven to 350°. Prepare crust by putting flour and salt in bowl of food processor. Add the butter and shortening and process, a few seconds at a time until mixture resembles coarse meal. Drop in ice water, a little at a time, until dough forms. Wrap and chill for an hour. Remove from refrigerator and let stand 15 minutes before rolling out. Line the bottom of a pie pan with rolled-out dough. Bake for approximately 20 minutes until golden brown and let cool.

Sprinkle strawberries with a few spoons of sugar and place them in the cooked shell. Pour the soda mixture over the strawberries and allow to set for 1 hour. Serve cold with whipped cream.

Classic Peanut Brittle

3½ cups granulated sugar
1 cup light corn syrup
2 cups water
¼ cup butter
1 lb raw peanuts
¼ tsp salt
1 tsp baking soda
1 Tbsp cold water

In a large pan, combine sugar, syrup and water. Cook over medium heat until sugar is dissolved, stirring constantly. Add butter and peanuts. Continue cooking, covered, for 2 minutes to wash down sugar crystals from sides of pan. Remove cover and cook until mixture reaches 300° on a candy thermometer. Remove from heat. Combine salt, baking soda, and tablespoon cold water and quickly stir into hot mixture. Pour into buttered jelly roll pan (about 11 x 17 inch). Cool and break into pieces. Makes about 3 pounds.

Flo's Favorite Fudge

4 Tbsp cocoa powder
2 cups extra fine sugar
4 Tbsp peanut butter
½ lb margarine or butter

Mix the cocoa and sugar together until fully mixed. In a double boiler, melt the butter and peanut butter together. Pour into bowl with sugar-cocoa mix. Mix well by hand. Grease a 9 x 9 pan. Place the fudge mixture into the pan and pat down until evenly distributed. Cut the fudge into squares and then refrigerate until firm. Let fudge warm up to room temperature before serving.